50 Craft Beer and Food Pairing Ideas

By: Kelly Johnson

Table of Contents

- IPA with Spicy Buffalo Wings
- Pale Ale with Grilled Salmon
- Stout with Chocolate Lava Cake
- Porter with BBQ Ribs
- Wheat Beer with Lemon Herb Grilled Chicken
- Saison with Goat Cheese Salad
- Amber Ale with Beef Tacos
- Brown Ale with Mushroom Risotto
- Sour Ale with Pickled Vegetables
- Barleywine with Blue Cheese
- Belgian Dubbel with Roast Duck
- Pilsner with Fish and Chips
- Cream Ale with Fried Calamari
- Session IPA with Grilled Shrimp Skewers
- Fruit Beer with Cheesecake
- Dunkel with Pretzels and Mustard
- Rye IPA with Spicy Sausage Pizza
- Hefeweizen with Banana Bread
- Bock with Pork Schnitzel
- Belgian Tripel with Spicy Thai Curry
- Amber Lager with BBQ Pulled Pork Sandwiches
- Cucumber Mint Gose with Light Salads
- West Coast IPA with Spicy Fish Tacos
- Imperial Stout with Espresso Brownies
- Fruit Lambic with Sorbet
- Brown Porter with Dark Chocolate Truffles
- Pale Ale with Grilled Vegetable Platter
- Black IPA with Charred Steak
- Saison with Quiche Lorraine
- Barleywine with Caramel Bread Pudding
- Belgian Blonde Ale with Garlic Shrimp
- Cascadian Dark Ale with BBQ Chicken Wings
- Kölsch with Smoked Salmon
- Doppelbock with Chocolate Chip Cookies
- Hazy IPA with Fried Chicken

- Raspberry Berliner Weisse with Cream Puffs
- Cream Stout with Irish Coffee Cake
- Sour Red Ale with Beef and Mushroom Stew
- American Wheat Beer with Fruit Salad
- Nitro Stout with Vanilla Ice Cream
- Bitter Ale with Caramelized Onions and Brie
- English Mild Ale with Bangers and Mash
- Citrus Pale Ale with Grilled Corn Salad
- Session Lager with Chicken Caesar Salad
- Spiced Ale with Pumpkin Pie
- Coconut Porter with Pecan Pie
- Smoked Porter with BBQ Brisket
- Vienna Lager with Chicken Enchiladas
- Saison with Herbed Goat Cheese
- Lambic with Almond Biscotti

IPA with Spicy Buffalo Wings

Ingredients:

- 2 pounds chicken wings
- 1 tablespoon baking powder
- 1 teaspoon salt
- 1 teaspoon garlic powder
- 1 teaspoon paprika
- 1/2 teaspoon cayenne pepper (adjust to taste)
- 1/2 cup hot sauce (e.g., Frank's RedHot)
- 4 tablespoons unsalted butter, melted
- Fresh celery sticks and blue cheese dressing for serving

Instructions:

1. Preheat your oven to 425°F (220°C) and line a baking sheet with aluminum foil. Place a wire rack on top of the baking sheet.
2. In a large bowl, toss the chicken wings with baking powder, salt, garlic powder, paprika, and cayenne pepper until evenly coated.
3. Arrange the wings in a single layer on the wire rack.
4. Bake for 40-45 minutes, turning halfway through, until the wings are crispy and golden brown.
5. While the wings bake, combine the hot sauce and melted butter in a small bowl.
6. Once the wings are done, toss them in the hot sauce mixture until well coated.
7. Serve with celery sticks and blue cheese dressing alongside your favorite IPA.

Pale Ale with Grilled Salmon

Ingredients:

- 4 salmon fillets (about 6 ounces each)
- 2 tablespoons olive oil
- 2 tablespoons lemon juice
- 2 teaspoons garlic, minced
- 1 teaspoon dried oregano
- 1 teaspoon salt
- 1/2 teaspoon black pepper
- Lemon wedges for serving
- Fresh herbs (e.g., parsley or dill) for garnish

Instructions:

1. In a bowl, whisk together olive oil, lemon juice, minced garlic, oregano, salt, and black pepper.
2. Place the salmon fillets in a shallow dish or resealable plastic bag. Pour the marinade over the salmon, ensuring they are well coated. Marinate for 30 minutes in the refrigerator.
3. Preheat your grill to medium-high heat and lightly oil the grates to prevent sticking.
4. Remove the salmon from the marinade and let any excess drip off. Place the salmon fillets skin-side down on the grill.
5. Grill for 5-6 minutes on each side, or until the salmon flakes easily with a fork and has nice grill marks.
6. Serve the grilled salmon with lemon wedges and garnish with fresh herbs. Enjoy it with a chilled pale ale for a refreshing pairing.

Enjoy your cooking and pairing experience!

Stout with Chocolate Lava Cake

Ingredients:

- 1/2 cup unsalted butter
- 1 cup bittersweet chocolate chips
- 2 eggs
- 2 egg yolks
- 1/4 cup sugar
- 2 tablespoons all-purpose flour
- Pinch of salt
- Cocoa powder for dusting
- Stout beer for pairing

Instructions:

1. Preheat the oven to 425°F (220°C) and grease four ramekins. Dust them with cocoa powder.
2. In a microwave-safe bowl, melt the butter and chocolate chips together until smooth.
3. In another bowl, whisk together the eggs, egg yolks, and sugar until pale and thick.
4. Stir the melted chocolate into the egg mixture, then fold in the flour and salt until just combined.
5. Divide the batter evenly among the ramekins. Bake for 12-14 minutes until the edges are firm but the center is still soft.
6. Let the cakes cool for 1 minute, then invert onto plates. Serve warm, paired with a stout beer.

Porter with BBQ Ribs

Ingredients:

- 2 racks of baby back ribs
- 1 tablespoon paprika
- 1 tablespoon brown sugar
- 1 teaspoon garlic powder
- 1 teaspoon onion powder
- 1 teaspoon salt
- 1/2 teaspoon black pepper
- 1/2 teaspoon cayenne pepper (optional)
- 1 cup BBQ sauce
- 1 cup porter beer

Instructions:

1. Preheat the oven to 300°F (150°C). Mix paprika, brown sugar, garlic powder, onion powder, salt, black pepper, and cayenne pepper in a bowl.
2. Rub the spice mixture generously over the ribs.
3. Place the ribs on a baking sheet lined with foil and cover tightly with more foil. Bake for 2.5 to 3 hours.
4. In a saucepan, combine BBQ sauce and porter beer, simmering over medium heat until slightly thickened.
5. After baking, remove the foil and brush the ribs with the BBQ sauce mixture. Broil for 5-7 minutes until caramelized.
6. Serve hot with extra BBQ sauce on the side and a chilled porter.

Wheat Beer with Lemon Herb Grilled Chicken

Ingredients:

- 4 chicken breasts
- 1/4 cup olive oil
- 1/4 cup lemon juice
- 2 teaspoons garlic, minced
- 1 tablespoon fresh thyme, chopped
- 1 tablespoon fresh rosemary, chopped
- Salt and pepper to taste
- Lemon wedges for serving
- Wheat beer for pairing

Instructions:

1. In a bowl, whisk together olive oil, lemon juice, garlic, thyme, rosemary, salt, and pepper.
2. Add the chicken breasts to the marinade and let them marinate for at least 30 minutes in the refrigerator.
3. Preheat the grill to medium heat and lightly oil the grates.
4. Grill the chicken for 6-7 minutes on each side until fully cooked.
5. Serve the chicken with lemon wedges and pair it with a refreshing wheat beer.

Saison with Goat Cheese Salad

Ingredients:

- 4 cups mixed salad greens
- 1/2 cup goat cheese, crumbled
- 1/4 cup walnuts, toasted
- 1/2 cup dried cranberries
- 1/4 cup olive oil
- 2 tablespoons balsamic vinegar
- Salt and pepper to taste
- Saison beer for pairing

Instructions:

1. In a large bowl, combine salad greens, goat cheese, walnuts, and cranberries.
2. In a separate bowl, whisk together olive oil, balsamic vinegar, salt, and pepper to make the dressing.
3. Drizzle the dressing over the salad and toss gently.
4. Serve immediately with a glass of saison.

Amber Ale with Beef Tacos

Ingredients:

- 1 pound ground beef
- 1 tablespoon taco seasoning
- 8 small corn tortillas
- 1 cup shredded lettuce
- 1 cup diced tomatoes
- 1/2 cup shredded cheese (cheddar or Mexican blend)
- Salsa and sour cream for serving
- Amber ale for pairing

Instructions:

1. In a skillet over medium heat, cook the ground beef until browned. Drain excess fat and add taco seasoning, mixing well.
2. Warm the tortillas in a dry skillet or microwave.
3. Assemble the tacos by adding beef, lettuce, tomatoes, and cheese to each tortilla.
4. Serve with salsa and sour cream alongside an amber ale.

Brown Ale with Mushroom Risotto

Ingredients:

- 1 cup Arborio rice
- 4 cups vegetable or chicken broth
- 1 cup mushrooms, sliced (e.g., cremini or shiitake)
- 1/2 onion, chopped
- 2 cloves garlic, minced
- 1/2 cup white wine
- 1/2 cup grated Parmesan cheese
- 2 tablespoons butter
- Salt and pepper to taste
- Brown ale for pairing

Instructions:

1. In a saucepan, heat the broth over low heat.
2. In a large skillet, melt butter and sauté onions and garlic until translucent. Add mushrooms and cook until softened.
3. Stir in the Arborio rice and cook for 2 minutes. Add white wine and let it absorb.
4. Gradually add the warm broth, one ladle at a time, stirring until absorbed before adding more.
5. Once the rice is creamy and al dente, stir in Parmesan cheese and season with salt and pepper.
6. Serve hot with a chilled brown ale.

Sour Ale with Pickled Vegetables

Ingredients:

- 2 cups assorted vegetables (e.g., cucumbers, carrots, radishes)
- 1 cup water
- 1 cup white vinegar
- 1 tablespoon sugar
- 1 tablespoon salt
- 1 teaspoon mustard seeds
- 1 teaspoon peppercorns
- Sour ale for pairing

Instructions:

1. In a saucepan, combine water, vinegar, sugar, salt, mustard seeds, and peppercorns. Bring to a boil, then remove from heat.
2. Place the assorted vegetables in a jar and pour the hot pickling liquid over them. Let cool, then refrigerate for at least 24 hours before serving.
3. Serve the pickled vegetables as a tangy side with a refreshing sour ale.

Barleywine with Blue Cheese

Ingredients:

- 8 ounces blue cheese, crumbled
- Crackers or bread for serving
- Barleywine for pairing

Instructions:

1. Arrange the crumbled blue cheese on a platter.
2. Serve with an assortment of crackers or slices of bread.
3. Pair with a rich, malty barleywine for a delightful contrast.

Enjoy these delicious recipes along with your favorite beers!

Belgian Dubbel with Roast Duck

Ingredients:

- 1 whole duck (about 4-5 lbs)
- Salt and pepper to taste
- 1 tablespoon olive oil
- 1 cup Belgian Dubbel beer
- 2 cloves garlic, minced
- 1 teaspoon fresh thyme
- 1 teaspoon fresh rosemary

Instructions:

1. Preheat the oven to 350°F (175°C). Season the duck with salt and pepper inside and out.
2. In a large oven-safe skillet, heat olive oil over medium-high heat. Sear the duck on all sides until browned.
3. Add garlic, thyme, rosemary, and pour in the Belgian Dubbel beer.
4. Cover the skillet with foil and roast in the oven for 1.5 to 2 hours, basting occasionally, until the duck is cooked through and tender.
5. Let the duck rest for 10 minutes before carving. Serve with the pan juices and a glass of Belgian Dubbel.

Pilsner with Fish and Chips

Ingredients:

- 4 white fish fillets (cod, haddock, or your choice)
- 1 cup all-purpose flour
- 1 cup beer (pilsner)
- 1 teaspoon baking powder
- Salt and pepper to taste
- 4 large potatoes, cut into fries
- Oil for frying
- Lemon wedges for serving

Instructions:

1. Heat oil in a deep fryer or heavy pot to 350°F (175°C).
2. In a bowl, mix flour, baking powder, salt, and pepper. Gradually whisk in the pilsner until the batter is smooth.
3. Dip fish fillets in the batter and fry until golden brown, about 4-5 minutes. Remove and drain on paper towels.
4. Fry the potato fries until golden and crispy, about 5-7 minutes. Drain and season with salt.
5. Serve the fish and chips with lemon wedges and a chilled pilsner.

Cream Ale with Fried Calamari

Ingredients:

- 1 pound calamari, cleaned and cut into rings
- 1 cup buttermilk
- 1 cup all-purpose flour
- 1 teaspoon paprika
- 1 teaspoon garlic powder
- Salt and pepper to taste
- Oil for frying
- Lemon wedges for serving

Instructions:

1. Soak the calamari rings in buttermilk for at least 30 minutes.
2. In a bowl, mix flour, paprika, garlic powder, salt, and pepper.
3. Heat oil in a deep fryer or heavy pot to 350°F (175°C).
4. Dredge the soaked calamari in the flour mixture and fry in batches until golden brown, about 2-3 minutes. Drain on paper towels.
5. Serve with lemon wedges and a glass of cream ale.

Session IPA with Grilled Shrimp Skewers

Ingredients:

- 1 pound large shrimp, peeled and deveined
- 2 tablespoons olive oil
- 1 teaspoon garlic powder
- 1 teaspoon paprika
- Salt and pepper to taste
- Lemon wedges for serving
- Session IPA for pairing

Instructions:

1. In a bowl, toss the shrimp with olive oil, garlic powder, paprika, salt, and pepper.
2. Preheat the grill to medium-high heat and thread the shrimp onto skewers.
3. Grill the shrimp for 2-3 minutes on each side until opaque and cooked through.
4. Serve the skewers with lemon wedges alongside a session IPA.

Fruit Beer with Cheesecake

Ingredients for Cheesecake:

- 1 1/2 cups graham cracker crumbs
- 1/3 cup sugar
- 1/2 cup butter, melted
- 4 (8 oz) packages cream cheese, softened
- 1 cup sugar
- 1 teaspoon vanilla extract
- 4 large eggs
- 1 cup fruit beer (your choice)

Instructions:

1. Preheat the oven to 325°F (160°C). Mix graham cracker crumbs, sugar, and melted butter. Press into the bottom of a springform pan.
2. In a large bowl, beat cream cheese until smooth. Gradually add sugar and vanilla, then beat in the eggs one at a time.
3. Mix in the fruit beer until well combined. Pour the filling over the crust.
4. Bake for 55-60 minutes until set. Let cool, then refrigerate for at least 4 hours.
5. Serve chilled with a glass of fruit beer.

Dunkel with Pretzels and Mustard

Ingredients for Pretzels:

- 1 1/2 cups warm water
- 1 packet active dry yeast
- 4 cups all-purpose flour
- 1/4 cup sugar
- 1/4 cup melted butter
- 1 teaspoon salt
- Baking soda for boiling
- Coarse salt for sprinkling

Instructions:

1. In a bowl, dissolve yeast in warm water. Add sugar, melted butter, flour, and salt. Knead until smooth. Let rise for 1 hour.
2. Preheat the oven to 450°F (230°C). Boil water in a large pot and add baking soda.
3. Divide dough into pieces and shape into pretzels. Boil each pretzel for 30 seconds, then place on a baking sheet.
4. Sprinkle with coarse salt and bake for 12-15 minutes until golden brown.
5. Serve warm with mustard and a dunkel.

Rye IPA with Spicy Sausage Pizza

Ingredients for Pizza:

- 1 pizza crust (store-bought or homemade)
- 1 cup pizza sauce
- 2 cups shredded mozzarella cheese
- 1 pound spicy sausage, cooked and crumbled
- 1/2 cup sliced jalapeños (optional)
- Olive oil for drizzling

Instructions:

1. Preheat the oven according to pizza crust instructions (usually around 475°F/245°C).
2. Roll out the pizza crust and place it on a pizza stone or baking sheet.
3. Spread pizza sauce evenly over the crust. Sprinkle mozzarella cheese on top.
4. Add the cooked sausage and jalapeños if using. Drizzle with olive oil.
5. Bake for 12-15 minutes until the crust is golden and cheese is bubbly.
6. Slice and serve with a cold rye IPA.

Hefeweizen with Banana Bread

Ingredients for Banana Bread:

- 3 ripe bananas, mashed
- 1/3 cup melted butter
- 1 teaspoon baking soda
- Pinch of salt
- 3/4 cup sugar
- 1 large egg, beaten
- 1 teaspoon vanilla extract
- 1 cup all-purpose flour

Instructions:

1. Preheat the oven to 350°F (175°C). Grease a loaf pan.
2. In a mixing bowl, mix the mashed bananas with melted butter. Stir in baking soda and salt.
3. Add sugar, beaten egg, and vanilla, mixing well. Stir in flour until just combined.
4. Pour the batter into the prepared loaf pan. Bake for 50-60 minutes until a toothpick inserted comes out clean.
5. Let cool before slicing and serve with a hefeweizen.

Enjoy these delicious recipes paired with your favorite beers!

Bock with Pork Schnitzel

Ingredients for Pork Schnitzel:

- 4 boneless pork chops, pounded thin
- Salt and pepper to taste
- 1 cup all-purpose flour
- 2 large eggs, beaten
- 1 cup breadcrumbs
- Oil for frying
- Lemon wedges for serving

Instructions:

1. Season the pork chops with salt and pepper. Dredge each chop in flour, dip in beaten eggs, and coat with breadcrumbs.
2. Heat oil in a large skillet over medium-high heat. Fry the schnitzels until golden brown on both sides, about 4-5 minutes per side. Drain on paper towels.
3. Serve the schnitzels with lemon wedges alongside a cold bock.

Belgian Tripel with Spicy Thai Curry

Ingredients for Spicy Thai Curry:

- 1 tablespoon vegetable oil
- 1 onion, chopped
- 2 cloves garlic, minced
- 1 tablespoon red curry paste
- 1 can (14 oz) coconut milk
- 1 cup vegetable or chicken broth
- 1 cup mixed vegetables (bell peppers, carrots, snap peas)
- 1 pound protein (chicken, tofu, or shrimp)
- Fresh basil for garnish
- Cooked rice for serving

Instructions:

1. Heat oil in a large pot over medium heat. Add onion and garlic, sautéing until soft.
2. Stir in the red curry paste and cook for 1-2 minutes until fragrant.
3. Add coconut milk and broth, bringing to a simmer. Add the mixed vegetables and protein, cooking until the protein is done and vegetables are tender.
4. Serve the curry over rice and garnish with fresh basil. Pair with a Belgian Tripel.

Amber Lager with BBQ Pulled Pork Sandwiches

Ingredients for Pulled Pork:

- 2 pounds pork shoulder
- 1 tablespoon paprika
- 1 tablespoon brown sugar
- 1 teaspoon garlic powder
- 1 teaspoon onion powder
- 1 cup BBQ sauce
- Sandwich buns for serving

Instructions:

1. Mix paprika, brown sugar, garlic powder, onion powder, salt, and pepper. Rub the mixture all over the pork shoulder.
2. Slow-cook the pork in a crockpot on low for 8 hours or until tender. Shred the pork and mix with BBQ sauce.
3. Serve on sandwich buns and enjoy with an amber lager.

Cucumber Mint Gose with Light Salads

Ingredients for Light Salad:

- 4 cups mixed greens
- 1 cucumber, sliced
- 1 cup cherry tomatoes, halved
- 1/4 cup red onion, thinly sliced
- 1/4 cup feta cheese, crumbled
- 1/4 cup olive oil
- 2 tablespoons red wine vinegar
- Salt and pepper to taste

Instructions:

1. In a large bowl, combine mixed greens, cucumber, cherry tomatoes, red onion, and feta cheese.
2. In a small bowl, whisk together olive oil, red wine vinegar, salt, and pepper. Drizzle over the salad and toss to combine.
3. Serve alongside a refreshing cucumber mint gose.

West Coast IPA with Spicy Fish Tacos

Ingredients for Spicy Fish Tacos:

- 1 pound white fish fillets (cod or tilapia)
- 1 tablespoon olive oil
- 1 teaspoon chili powder
- 1 teaspoon cumin
- Salt and pepper to taste
- Corn tortillas
- Cabbage slaw (cabbage, lime juice, cilantro)
- Avocado slices

Instructions:

1. Preheat the grill or skillet over medium-high heat. Toss fish with olive oil, chili powder, cumin, salt, and pepper.
2. Grill or pan-fry the fish until cooked through, about 3-4 minutes per side. Flake into pieces.
3. Serve in corn tortillas topped with cabbage slaw and avocado slices. Enjoy with a West Coast IPA.

Imperial Stout with Espresso Brownies

Ingredients for Espresso Brownies:

- 1/2 cup butter
- 1 cup sugar
- 2 large eggs
- 1 teaspoon vanilla extract
- 1/2 cup all-purpose flour
- 1/3 cup cocoa powder
- 1/4 teaspoon salt
- 1 tablespoon instant espresso powder
- 1/2 cup chocolate chips

Instructions:

1. Preheat the oven to 350°F (175°C). Grease an 8x8-inch baking pan.
2. Melt butter in a saucepan. Stir in sugar, eggs, and vanilla. Mix in flour, cocoa powder, salt, and espresso powder until combined. Fold in chocolate chips.
3. Pour the batter into the prepared pan and bake for 20-25 minutes until set. Let cool before cutting into squares.
4. Serve with a glass of rich imperial stout.

Fruit Lambic with Sorbet

Ingredients for Sorbet:

- 4 cups fruit (such as strawberries, mangoes, or raspberries)
- 1 cup sugar
- 1 cup water
- 1 tablespoon lemon juice

Instructions:

1. In a saucepan, combine sugar and water, bringing to a boil until sugar dissolves. Let cool.
2. Puree the fruit in a blender and mix in the cooled syrup and lemon juice.
3. Pour the mixture into an ice cream maker and churn according to manufacturer's instructions. If you don't have an ice cream maker, freeze in a shallow container, stirring every 30 minutes until firm.
4. Serve the sorbet alongside a refreshing fruit lambic.

Brown Porter with Dark Chocolate Truffles

Ingredients for Dark Chocolate Truffles:

- 8 ounces dark chocolate, chopped
- 1/2 cup heavy cream
- Cocoa powder for dusting

Instructions:

1. In a small saucepan, heat heavy cream until just simmering. Pour over the chopped chocolate and let sit for 5 minutes, then stir until smooth.
2. Chill the mixture in the refrigerator until firm, about 1-2 hours. Scoop small amounts and roll into balls.
3. Dust the truffles with cocoa powder and serve with a glass of brown porter.

Enjoy these delicious pairings and recipes!

Pale Ale with Grilled Vegetable Platter

Ingredients for Grilled Vegetable Platter:

- 1 zucchini, sliced
- 1 bell pepper, cut into strips
- 1 eggplant, sliced
- 1 red onion, cut into wedges
- 1 cup cherry tomatoes
- 2 tablespoons olive oil
- Salt and pepper to taste
- Fresh herbs (such as basil or thyme) for garnish

Instructions:

1. Preheat the grill to medium-high heat. In a large bowl, toss the vegetables with olive oil, salt, and pepper.
2. Grill the vegetables for 4-5 minutes per side, or until tender and slightly charred.
3. Arrange the grilled vegetables on a platter and garnish with fresh herbs. Serve with a cold pale ale.

Black IPA with Charred Steak

Ingredients for Charred Steak:

- 2 ribeye or sirloin steaks
- Salt and pepper to taste
- 2 tablespoons olive oil
- 1 teaspoon smoked paprika
- Fresh herbs (such as rosemary or thyme) for garnish

Instructions:

1. Preheat the grill to high heat. Season the steaks with salt, pepper, olive oil, and smoked paprika.
2. Grill the steaks for about 4-5 minutes per side for medium-rare, adjusting the time based on desired doneness.
3. Let the steaks rest for a few minutes, then slice and garnish with fresh herbs. Enjoy with a black IPA.

Saison with Quiche Lorraine

Ingredients for Quiche Lorraine:

- 1 pie crust (store-bought or homemade)
- 6 large eggs
- 1 cup heavy cream
- 1 cup shredded Swiss cheese
- 1 cup diced cooked bacon
- 1/2 cup chopped green onions
- Salt and pepper to taste

Instructions:

1. Preheat the oven to 375°F (190°C). Place the pie crust in a pie dish and pre-bake for 10 minutes.
2. In a bowl, whisk together the eggs, heavy cream, salt, and pepper. Stir in the cheese, bacon, and green onions.
3. Pour the egg mixture into the pre-baked crust. Bake for 30-35 minutes, or until the quiche is set and lightly browned.
4. Let cool slightly before slicing. Serve warm with a saison.

Barleywine with Caramel Bread Pudding

Ingredients for Caramel Bread Pudding:

- 4 cups stale bread, cubed
- 4 large eggs
- 2 cups milk
- 1 cup heavy cream
- 1 cup brown sugar
- 1 teaspoon vanilla extract
- 1/2 cup caramel sauce

Instructions:

1. Preheat the oven to 350°F (175°C). Grease a baking dish.
2. In a large bowl, whisk together eggs, milk, cream, brown sugar, and vanilla extract. Add the bread cubes, allowing them to soak for 15 minutes.
3. Pour the mixture into the prepared baking dish and bake for 40-45 minutes, or until set and golden.
4. Drizzle with caramel sauce before serving. Enjoy with a glass of barleywine.

Belgian Blonde Ale with Garlic Shrimp

Ingredients for Garlic Shrimp:

- 1 pound large shrimp, peeled and deveined
- 4 cloves garlic, minced
- 2 tablespoons olive oil
- 1 tablespoon lemon juice
- Salt and pepper to taste
- Fresh parsley for garnish

Instructions:

1. In a large skillet, heat olive oil over medium heat. Add garlic and sauté for 1 minute until fragrant.
2. Add the shrimp, salt, and pepper, cooking until the shrimp turn pink, about 3-4 minutes.
3. Stir in lemon juice and garnish with fresh parsley. Serve with a Belgian blonde ale.

Cascadian Dark Ale with BBQ Chicken Wings

Ingredients for BBQ Chicken Wings:

- 2 pounds chicken wings
- 1/2 cup BBQ sauce
- Salt and pepper to taste
- Optional: fresh herbs for garnish

Instructions:

1. Preheat the oven to 400°F (200°C). Season chicken wings with salt and pepper.
2. Place wings on a baking sheet and bake for 30-35 minutes, turning halfway through, until crispy.
3. Toss the wings in BBQ sauce and return to the oven for an additional 5-10 minutes.
4. Serve hot with a cascadian dark ale.

Kölsch with Smoked Salmon

Ingredients for Smoked Salmon Platter:

- 8 ounces smoked salmon
- 1 tablespoon capers
- 1/2 red onion, thinly sliced
- Fresh dill for garnish
- Lemon wedges for serving
- Cream cheese or crème fraîche (optional)

Instructions:

1. Arrange the smoked salmon on a platter. Top with capers, red onion slices, and fresh dill.
2. Serve with lemon wedges and cream cheese or crème fraîche if desired. Pair with a refreshing kölsch.

Doppelbock with Chocolate Chip Cookies

Ingredients for Chocolate Chip Cookies:

- 1 cup unsalted butter, softened
- 1 cup brown sugar
- 1/2 cup granulated sugar
- 2 large eggs
- 1 teaspoon vanilla extract
- 2 1/4 cups all-purpose flour
- 1 teaspoon baking soda
- 1/2 teaspoon salt
- 2 cups chocolate chips

Instructions:

1. Preheat the oven to 350°F (175°C). Line a baking sheet with parchment paper.
2. In a large bowl, cream together the butter, brown sugar, and granulated sugar. Beat in the eggs and vanilla.
3. In a separate bowl, whisk together flour, baking soda, and salt. Gradually add to the butter mixture, mixing until combined. Fold in chocolate chips.
4. Drop spoonfuls of dough onto the prepared baking sheet. Bake for 10-12 minutes until golden. Let cool on a wire rack.
5. Enjoy warm cookies with a doppelbock.

Enjoy these delicious pairings and recipes!

Hazy IPA with Fried Chicken

Ingredients for Fried Chicken:

- 4 chicken pieces (legs, thighs, or breasts)
- 1 cup buttermilk
- 1 cup all-purpose flour
- 1 teaspoon paprika
- 1 teaspoon garlic powder
- Salt and pepper to taste
- Oil for frying

Instructions:

1. In a bowl, marinate chicken in buttermilk for at least 2 hours or overnight in the fridge.
2. In a separate bowl, mix flour, paprika, garlic powder, salt, and pepper.
3. Heat oil in a large skillet over medium heat. Dredge marinated chicken in the flour mixture and fry until golden brown and cooked through, about 10-12 minutes per side.
4. Drain on paper towels. Serve hot with a refreshing hazy IPA.

Raspberry Berliner Weisse with Cream Puffs

Ingredients for Cream Puffs:

- 1 cup water
- 1/2 cup unsalted butter
- 1 cup all-purpose flour
- 4 large eggs
- 1 teaspoon vanilla extract
- 1 cup heavy cream
- 2 tablespoons powdered sugar

Instructions:

1. Preheat the oven to 400°F (200°C). Line a baking sheet with parchment paper.
2. In a saucepan, combine water and butter. Bring to a boil, then add flour and stir until the mixture forms a ball. Remove from heat and let cool slightly.
3. Beat in eggs one at a time, mixing until smooth. Add vanilla extract.
4. Pipe or spoon small mounds of dough onto the baking sheet. Bake for 20-25 minutes until golden.
5. Let cool, then whip the cream with powdered sugar. Fill the cooled puffs with whipped cream.
6. Serve with a chilled raspberry Berliner Weisse.

Cream Stout with Irish Coffee Cake

Ingredients for Irish Coffee Cake:

- 1 cup unsalted butter, softened
- 1 cup granulated sugar
- 1 cup brown sugar
- 4 large eggs
- 2 cups all-purpose flour
- 1/2 cup cocoa powder
- 1 teaspoon baking powder
- 1 teaspoon baking soda
- 1/2 teaspoon salt
- 1 cup brewed coffee
- 1/2 cup Irish cream liqueur

Instructions:

1. Preheat the oven to 350°F (175°C). Grease a bundt pan.
2. In a large bowl, cream together butter, granulated sugar, and brown sugar until fluffy. Add eggs one at a time.
3. In another bowl, mix flour, cocoa powder, baking powder, baking soda, and salt. Gradually add dry ingredients to the wet mixture, alternating with brewed coffee and Irish cream.
4. Pour into the prepared bundt pan and bake for 45-50 minutes. Let cool before removing from the pan.
5. Serve slices with a glass of cream stout.

Sour Red Ale with Beef and Mushroom Stew

Ingredients for Beef and Mushroom Stew:

- 2 pounds beef chuck, cut into cubes
- 1 cup mushrooms, sliced
- 1 onion, chopped
- 2 carrots, diced
- 2 cloves garlic, minced
- 4 cups beef broth
- 1 cup sour red ale
- 2 tablespoons tomato paste
- 2 teaspoons dried thyme
- Salt and pepper to taste

Instructions:

1. In a large pot, brown the beef cubes over medium heat. Remove and set aside.
2. In the same pot, add onions, carrots, and garlic, cooking until softened. Stir in mushrooms and cook for another 2 minutes.
3. Add the beef back into the pot along with beef broth, sour red ale, tomato paste, thyme, salt, and pepper. Bring to a boil.
4. Reduce heat and simmer for 1.5 to 2 hours, until the beef is tender. Serve hot with a sour red ale.

American Wheat Beer with Fruit Salad

Ingredients for Fruit Salad:

- 1 cup strawberries, sliced
- 1 cup blueberries
- 1 cup kiwi, diced
- 1 cup pineapple, diced
- 1 cup melon, diced
- 2 tablespoons honey or maple syrup
- Juice of 1 lime

Instructions:

1. In a large bowl, combine all the fruit.
2. Drizzle with honey (or maple syrup) and lime juice. Toss gently to combine.
3. Serve chilled alongside a refreshing American wheat beer.

Nitro Stout with Vanilla Ice Cream

Ingredients for Vanilla Ice Cream:

- 2 cups heavy cream
- 1 cup whole milk
- 3/4 cup granulated sugar
- 1 tablespoon vanilla extract
- Pinch of salt

Instructions:

1. In a bowl, whisk together cream, milk, sugar, vanilla extract, and salt until sugar is dissolved.
2. Pour the mixture into an ice cream maker and churn according to the manufacturer's instructions.
3. Freeze for at least 4 hours or until firm.
4. Serve scoops of vanilla ice cream topped with a rich nitro stout.

Bitter Ale with Caramelized Onions and Brie

Ingredients for Caramelized Onions and Brie:

- 2 large onions, thinly sliced
- 2 tablespoons butter
- Salt to taste
- 8 ounces brie cheese, sliced
- Baguette slices for serving

Instructions:

1. In a skillet, melt butter over medium heat. Add onions and a pinch of salt, cooking slowly until caramelized, about 20-30 minutes.
2. Preheat the oven to 350°F (175°C). Place sliced brie on a baking sheet.
3. Bake for 5-10 minutes until brie is soft and melted.
4. Top the brie with caramelized onions and serve warm with baguette slices and a glass of bitter ale.

English Mild Ale with Bangers and Mash

Ingredients for Bangers and Mash:

- 4 pork sausages
- 2 pounds potatoes, peeled and diced
- 1/2 cup milk
- 4 tablespoons butter
- Salt and pepper to taste
- Gravy for serving (optional)

Instructions:

1. Boil potatoes in salted water until tender, about 15-20 minutes. Drain and mash with milk, butter, salt, and pepper.
2. In a skillet, cook sausages over medium heat until browned and cooked through.
3. Serve sausages on a bed of mashed potatoes, drizzled with gravy if desired, alongside an English mild ale.

Enjoy these delicious pairings and recipes!

Citrus Pale Ale with Grilled Corn Salad

Ingredients for Grilled Corn Salad:

- 4 ears of corn, husked
- 1 red bell pepper, diced
- 1/4 red onion, finely chopped
- 1 cup cherry tomatoes, halved
- 1 avocado, diced
- 1/4 cup fresh cilantro, chopped
- Juice of 2 limes
- 2 tablespoons olive oil
- Salt and pepper to taste

Instructions:

1. Preheat the grill to medium-high heat. Grill the corn, turning occasionally, until charred and cooked through, about 10 minutes. Let cool, then cut the kernels off the cob.
2. In a large bowl, combine grilled corn, red bell pepper, red onion, cherry tomatoes, avocado, and cilantro.
3. Drizzle with lime juice and olive oil, and season with salt and pepper. Toss gently to combine.
4. Serve chilled or at room temperature with a refreshing citrus pale ale.

Session Lager with Chicken Caesar Salad

Ingredients for Chicken Caesar Salad:

- 2 grilled chicken breasts, sliced
- 6 cups romaine lettuce, chopped
- 1/2 cup Caesar dressing
- 1/2 cup croutons
- 1/4 cup grated Parmesan cheese
- Freshly ground black pepper to taste

Instructions:

1. In a large bowl, combine romaine lettuce, sliced chicken, Caesar dressing, croutons, and Parmesan cheese.
2. Toss gently until the salad is evenly coated.
3. Season with freshly ground black pepper and serve with a chilled session lager.

Spiced Ale with Pumpkin Pie

Ingredients for Pumpkin Pie:

- 1 (15 oz) can pumpkin puree
- 3/4 cup sugar
- 1/2 teaspoon salt
- 1 teaspoon ground cinnamon
- 1 teaspoon ground ginger
- 1/2 teaspoon ground nutmeg
- 1/4 teaspoon ground cloves
- 3 large eggs
- 1 (9-inch) unbaked pie crust

Instructions:

1. Preheat the oven to 425°F (220°C).
2. In a large bowl, mix pumpkin puree, sugar, salt, spices, and eggs until smooth. Pour into the pie crust.
3. Bake for 15 minutes, then reduce the temperature to 350°F (175°C) and bake for an additional 35-40 minutes until the filling is set.
4. Cool before serving with a spiced ale.

Coconut Porter with Pecan Pie

Ingredients for Pecan Pie:

- 1 pie crust (homemade or store-bought)
- 1 cup corn syrup

- 1 cup brown sugar
- 1/4 cup melted butter
- 3 large eggs
- 1 teaspoon vanilla extract
- 2 cups pecan halves

Instructions:

1. Preheat the oven to 350°F (175°C). Fit the pie crust into a 9-inch pie plate.
2. In a bowl, mix corn syrup, brown sugar, melted butter, eggs, and vanilla until well combined. Stir in pecans.
3. Pour the filling into the pie crust and bake for 60-70 minutes until set.
4. Let cool before serving with a rich coconut porter.

Smoked Porter with BBQ Brisket

Ingredients for BBQ Brisket:

- 3-4 pounds beef brisket
- 2 tablespoons smoked paprika
- 2 tablespoons brown sugar
- 1 tablespoon garlic powder
- 1 tablespoon onion powder
- 1 tablespoon salt
- 1 teaspoon black pepper
- BBQ sauce for serving

Instructions:

1. Preheat the oven to 300°F (150°C).
2. In a bowl, mix smoked paprika, brown sugar, garlic powder, onion powder, salt, and pepper. Rub the spice mixture all over the brisket.
3. Place the brisket in a roasting pan and cover with foil. Roast for 3-4 hours until tender.
4. Remove from the oven, let rest, and slice. Serve with BBQ sauce and a smoked porter.

Vienna Lager with Chicken Enchiladas

Ingredients for Chicken Enchiladas:

- 2 cups cooked chicken, shredded
- 1 cup shredded cheese (cheddar or Mexican blend)
- 1 can (10 oz) enchilada sauce
- 8 small flour or corn tortillas
- 1/4 cup sour cream (for serving)
- Fresh cilantro for garnish

Instructions:

1. Preheat the oven to 350°F (175°C). Grease a baking dish.
2. In a bowl, combine shredded chicken, 1/2 cup cheese, and 1/2 cup enchilada sauce.
3. Fill each tortilla with the chicken mixture, roll up, and place seam-side down in the baking dish.
4. Pour the remaining enchilada sauce over the top and sprinkle with remaining cheese.
5. Bake for 20-25 minutes until cheese is melted. Serve with sour cream and a Vienna lager.

Saison with Herbed Goat Cheese

Ingredients for Herbed Goat Cheese:

- 8 oz goat cheese, softened
- 2 tablespoons fresh herbs (such as chives, thyme, and parsley), finely chopped
- 1 tablespoon olive oil
- Salt and pepper to taste
- Crackers or baguette slices for serving

Instructions:

1. In a bowl, mix softened goat cheese, fresh herbs, olive oil, salt, and pepper until well combined.
2. Form into a log or ball and wrap in plastic wrap. Chill for at least 30 minutes to firm up.
3. Serve with crackers or baguette slices alongside a refreshing saison.

Lambic with Almond Biscotti

Ingredients for Almond Biscotti:

- 2 cups all-purpose flour
- 1 cup granulated sugar
- 1 teaspoon baking powder
- 1/2 teaspoon salt
- 3 large eggs
- 1 teaspoon vanilla extract
- 1 cup sliced almonds

Instructions:

1. Preheat the oven to 350°F (175°C). Line a baking sheet with parchment paper.
2. In a bowl, mix flour, sugar, baking powder, and salt. In another bowl, whisk together eggs and vanilla extract.
3. Combine wet and dry ingredients, then fold in sliced almonds.
4. Divide dough in half and shape into logs. Place on the baking sheet and bake for 25 minutes.
5. Let cool slightly, then slice into biscotti shapes and bake for an additional 10-15 minutes until golden.
6. Serve with a sweet lambic.

Enjoy these delicious pairings and recipes!